THE RICHES OF CHRIST

WHAT TRUE PROSPERITY LOOKS LIKE

The Riches of Christ: What True Posperity Looks Like

Contents of this book are excerpted from *True Prosperity*, copyright © 2004 by James Robison. All rights reserved.

Copyright© 2017 by Inprov, Ltd.
ISBN: 978-0-9963685-8-2

For further information, write Inprov, at:
2150 E. Continental Blvd, Southlake, TX 76092

CONTENTS

INTRODUCTION

Over the past fifty years I have spoken with many people who have achieved true prosperity in life. I want to share with you what I learned from them. Also, the Lord has shown me many things in life—choices made, attitudes maintained, temptations resisted, relationships developed—that lead to true prosperity. I have put these key elements in writing to help you realize the blessings the Lord has in store for you.

Sometimes just a few simple ideas can completely change your life. For example, learning how to be a river instead of a reservoir. Or learning how to *scale down* in order to *step up*. Or perhaps you need to learn how to identify and remove major obstacles to prosperity.

The truths that I share in this book come with the confidence that God's will is to bless you beyond anything you could ever imagine—not just monetarily but in ways that are priceless!

James Robison

James Robison

WHAT IS TRUE PROSPERITY?

I believe that our loving heavenly Father wants to bless us in this lifetime. I believe it because I read it in His Word, and I know it is true because I have experienced it in my own life and have observed it clearly in the lives of many others.

Over the years I have earnestly sought answers from

God and in His Word in order to share some realistic answers to key questions about true prosperity:

- Amid the circumstances of life, why are Betty and I so blessed and full of peace?
- How did I, a boy as the product of a forced sexual relationship and raised in poverty, find such success, personal joy, and even monetary blessing?
- Can everyone enjoy the same spiritual, emotional, and material prosperity that I have?
- Can I share God's truth that will help others find true prosperity?

We must move beyond thinking of prosperity in purely monetary or materialistic terms. Limiting our concept of abundance to finances ignores the wealth of time, gifts, and abilities that mark truly successful people.

If you have bought into the idea that God—or life— owes you something and you're getting the short end of the stick, then you have constructed a major roadblock in your path to prosperity. Covetousness and resentment block your ability to see clearly and discern wisely. These issues must be rooted out and dealt with.

It is my deep conviction that deliverance from these

unhealthy attitudes and thoughts clears a person's mind to exercise sound judgment and make wise decisions, including those related to investments and financial opportunity.

True prosperity is having all the resources we need to fulfill God's purpose for our lives and the abiding peace and joy that enable us to be perfectly content in abundance or while facing grave challenges.

God desires to bless everyone . . . He wants us to continually experience His boundless, limitless love. God has promised to meet our needs, but we must understand that He is the One who accurately defines our needs.

The sooner we learn the following truth, the happier we will be: **if you want to experience life fully, begin to express life freely.**

It is our responsibility to help feed the hungry, give water to the thirsty, clothe the naked, and share the love of Jesus Christ. That is a major purpose of our prosperity.

Society tells us that happiness and fulfillment come through consumerism—buying. In other words, the key to life is getting. This flies in the face of the wisdom imparted by the greatest teacher who ever walked the planet.

He said, "It is more blessed to give than to receive" (Acts 20:35, NKJV).

Instead of seeking prosperity, seek God's perfect will for your life! When you trust Him and His plan, prosperity will find you.

True Prosperity.

I AM NOT SAYING THIS BECAUSE I AM IN NEED, FOR I HAVE LEARNED TO BE CONTENT WHATEVER THE CIRCUMSTANCES. I KNOW WHAT IT IS TO BE IN NEED, AND I KNOW WHAT IT IS TO HAVE PLENTY. I HAVE LEARNED THE SECRET OF BEING CONTENT IN ANY AND EVERY SITUATION, WHETHER WELL FED OR HUNGRY, WHETHER LIVING IN PLENTY OR IN WANT.

Philippians 4:11-12 (NIV)

Dr. Tony Evans has been a guest on our television program, *LIFE TODAY*, numerous times. Once, as we were discussing his book *God Is More Than Enough*, I said to the television audience, "You're really going to get blessed when you bless others. Isn't that right, Tony?" "Absolutely," Dr. Evans replied. "You can't outgive God." "That doesn't mean he's going to give you a money tree, though." I said. "He's going to give you what money can't buy." Then Dr. Evans uttered a short but profound statement that captures the essence of true prosperity:

"He's going to give you Himself."

That is the wealth that God promises: riches in Christ.

We don't focus our attention on
the expected harvest, although we
know it will come in due season.
Our joy comes through the act
of giving—giving of our time, our
talent, our wisdom, our finances,
and every good thing that comes
from the Father above.

PROSPERITY . . .

Prosperity is more than finances.

It is the blessings of God poured out over our lives and manifested in a multitude of areas!

You may prosper in your finances, but you can also prosper in your spiritual gifts, your relationships, your work performance, or any other area of your life.

Today we ask for a spirit of gratitude and humility. No matter how much or how little we have, we seek contentment in every circumstance like Paul—simply because of God and the strength we receive through Him. We are blessed beyond measure because of our heavenly Father. Let us not lose sight of what is important and continue to seek contentment. Amen.

When you love God with all your heart, you will begin to love your neighbor, and the outward expression of this relationship and commitment will be undeniable. You will share your time with others. By giving of your means and by using the talents God has given you, those around you will benefit and **you will bring God glory.**

AND HE ANSWERED, "YOU SHALL LOVE THE LORD YOUR GOD WITH ALL YOUR HEART, AND WITH ALL YOUR SOUL, AND WITH ALL YOUR STRENGTH, AND WITH ALL YOUR MIND; AND YOUR NEIGHBOR AS YOURSELF."

Luke 10:27 (NASB)

Once I was teaching the principles of giving in a church, and we were seeing a tremendous move of God's Spirit among the people. People were responding and giving to the church and to one another as the Lord led them.

One night, a couple who were seemingly broken before the Lord came up to me. They were weeping almost uncontrollably. They said that the Lord spoke to them about giving away every penny they had. I learned that they had written a check for all the money they had in the world. Now they were bringing me the check, saying, "We are supposed to give this to you. Do whatever you feel you're supposed to do with it."

Immediately, I knew what the Lord wanted me to do. When they handed me the check, I asked them, "Are you saying this is mine now, and I can do anything I want with it?" Through their tears they nodded and answered yes. So, I said, "Well, I know exactly what the Lord would have me to do with this check." Then I tore it up in front of them. Immediately, they fell to the floor and began to weep uncontrollably.

God did a wondrous work in their hearts that night—one that changed them for the rest of their lives. They were never the same. That incident reminds me of a spiritual principle that my wife and I have come to call the I.O. Principle. I.O. stands for Instant Obedience. We have come to understand the importance of responding instantly when we hear God's voice.

With that couple, I could have waited to see how much the check was for. I could have pocketed it, prayed about it further, and torn it up later. But that would've been dangerous.

Sometimes in giving, if you wait, Satan is given time to come up with all kinds of good reasons not to do what God has told you to do. The longer you wait, the more time there is for your mind and emotions to cloud the message.

If God speaks it, do it. Trust and obey. And do it now! Don't give Satan an opportunity to help you rationalize another course of action. Follow the I.O. Principle.

Excerpted from The Blessed Life *by Robert Morris (Regal Books). Robert's teaching is a part of the series, "More than Enough."*

JOY...

Jesus tells us that joy comes from being in God's presence. Joy is a heavenly fulfillment of contentedness and peace. We can enter into this joy when we participate as the body of Christ, reaching out to those around us in His great love and abundant provision. The joy of the Lord is our strength! True prosperity is "joy inexpressible and full of glory" (1 Peter 1:8, NASB).

PRAYER:

Lord, help us to be obedient to Your voice. When You call us to act, let us act on Your command. We pray that we are not tempted by hesitation or apprehension. We know that the enemy uses those feelings to manipulate us and keep us from acting according to Your will for our lives. Thank You for Your heavenly presence. Amen.

Father, help us remember that

joy can come through giving.

We want to share the good things we are blessed with, with those around us. Direct our attention to the needs of those in our lives. Show us what we can give to help meet those needs as directed by Your love and grace. And fill us with the joy that can only be experienced by giving.

REMEMBER, JESUS SAID, "DON'T WORRY," NOT, "DON'T WORK." BIRDS START EACH DAY EARLY, WORKING TO FIND WHAT GOD PROVIDES!

"THEREFORE I SAY TO YOU, DO NOT WORRY ABOUT YOUR LIFE, WHAT YOU WILL EAT OR WHAT YOU WILL DRINK; NOR ABOUT YOUR BODY, WHAT YOU WILL PUT ON. IS NOT LIFE MORE THAN FOOD AND THE BODY MORE THAN CLOTHING? LOOK AT THE BIRDS OF THE AIR, FOR THEY NEITHER SOW NOR REAP NOR GATHER INTO BARNS; YET YOUR HEAVENLY FATHER FEEDS THEM."

(Matthew 6:25-26, NKJV)

He wants us to trust Him for our provision, whether we are rich or poor. And He wants us to gladly and faithfully give our finances to help others, whether it is a million dollars or a widow's mite.

WHAT IS *NOT* TRUE PROSPERITY?

We can learn a lot about true prosperity by studying what true prosperity is not. By stripping away misunderstandings related to prosperity, we can get down to the reality of the prosperous life.

True prosperity is not merely the accumulation of material possessions or wealth . . . Although God often blesses believers with great material wealth, it is not necessarily a sign of spiritual depth or faith. In fact, Satan used material wealth and power to tempt Jesus Christ, claiming that he had the ability to give wealth (see Matthew 4:8-9).

The clear message throughout Scripture is that it is better to have just a little money and be on God's side than to have a lot of money and be apart from God. The real emphasis is on righteousness, which does not necessarily coincide with large amounts of money.

In the church we often see two extreme views. One says that Christians should have nothing; the other says that Christians should have it all. Somewhere, a biblical balance must be found. It's not about gaining monetary wealth; it's about learning to live with true prosperity and understanding what that actually means.

Prosperity is not wealth, power, fame, recognition, or comfort.

You may experience these things alongside prosperity, but having one or some of these does not guarantee prosperity through Christ.

You cannot know true prosperity without knowing God intimately. It is possible only when we are absolutely convinced that God—in whom we trust explicitly and exclusively—will "supply all your needs from his glorious riches" (Philippians 4:19, NLT).

True prosperity encompasses so much more than merely money. It includes having the time, the talent, the wisdom, and the wealth of God—as well as His presence . . .

Servants don't get much recognition, but through their service they have a positive impact on the lives of others. Parents often don't get recognition, but their reward comes through the meaningful and productive lives of their children. Missionaries often toil in complete obscurity, yet their reward comes through the souls they reach with the gospel of Jesus Christ.

The heart of a servant captures the essence of true prosperity.

"NOT SO WITH YOU. INSTEAD, WHOEVER WANTS TO BECOME GREAT AMONG YOU MUST BE YOUR SERVANT, AND WHOEVER WANTS TO BE FIRST MUST BE YOUR SLAVE— JUST AS THE SON OF MAN DID NOT COME TO BE SERVED, BUT TO SERVE, AND TO GIVE HIS LIFE AS A RANSOM FOR MANY."

Matthew 20:26-28 (NIV)

Peter Pretorius, a missionary who feeds starving people across the continent of Africa, says, regarding our giving to feed the hungry,

"We are not measured by how much we give to others, but rather how much we keep for ourselves."

Some of the more prosperous
individuals portrayed in the Bible
are people who suffered. The
apostle Paul was in prison, for
example, far from comfort, yet he
considered himself so prosperous
and free that he and his traveling
companion, Silas, sang praises to
God in the Philippian jail
(see Acts 16:23-25).

Comfort can be nice, but the inner
peace of true prosperity, which comes
by God's grace, is much better.

PEACE...

Many people choose to follow Christ at great risk to their welfare, reputation, possessions, and even their very lives. Betty and I have closely observed many missionaries who live sacrificially yet experience overwhelming joy and peace while also facing monumental challenges. There is a supernatural peace that falls over our lives when we pursue Christ. No matter what challenges we may face, God provides heavenly peace in our lives that brings fulfillment and contentment.

PRAYER:

Father, remind us that material possessions are temporary, but spiritual things are eternal. We were not only made for our short time on earth; we were made for our eternal life with You, God. Let our actions speak for our future, and help us to coach our minds away from the temporary, shifting our focus to the eternal. Amen.

Is it possible to be completely unnoticed, yet still prosperous? Gaining recognition in the world does not guarantee prosperity. It might increase your status, your wealth, your influence, or your responsibilities, but it does not automatically instill **inner peace and satisfaction.**

FOR YOU KNOW THE GRACE OF OUR LORD
JESUS CHRIST, THAT THOUGH HE WAS
RICH, YET FOR YOUR SAKE HE BECAME
POOR, SO THAT YOU THROUGH HIS
POVERTY MIGHT BECOME RICH.

2 Corinthians 8:9 (NIV)

Right from the start, James and I came to a crucial agreement, one we believe is supported by the words of the Bible. We agreed not to indulge in compulsive spending and not to try to impress people with any of the stuff we had. As James likes to say, **"It's okay to have stuff; it's not okay for stuff to have you." Never allow the things you possess to possess you.**

There simply isn't room in the Christian life to worry about impressing other people. We should never want anything because someone else has it or because it's a status symbol. There's nothing wrong with possessing the things you need or even the things you want. But how can you "take an interest in others" if you're drowning in debt?

Paul also tells us in Philippians that God will supply our needs. And he says in 2 Corinthians that if we learn to keep God first, even in our giving, He will enable us to give to every good work. In the book of Proverbs, we are told, "Honor the Lord with your possessions, and with the firstfruits of all your increase." When we keep God first, it's amazing how much better we manage our money.

The part of you that wants to impress people and revel in vanity—the part that wants to determine your personal worth based on your possessions—is the part that has to die. You will never be happy if you try to base who you are on what you have. This way of thinking leads only to dissatisfaction and a constant pursuit of "uncertain riches." When you build your self-worth on the foundation of money, you're foolishly building your house on an unstable foundation.

If you're currently pursuing or living for foolish material gain, we encourage you to take these thoughts and attitudes to the Lord and to start living under His control, not out of control. God wants the best for you, but His best often looks much different from what the world thinks is best.

Find your worth in God, and you'll experience true prosperity. Jesus promises us an abundance of life, which is not the same as an abundance of possessions. If, however, you keep first things first, you can and will enjoy all things richly.

From Living in Love *by James and Betty Robison.*

RICHNESS ...

The more important lesson we learn about riches from examining the life of Christ is this: **it's not about getting rich—it's about living richly.**

Christ's life shows us that there is a beautiful richness that comes when we live a life of serving others and loving deeply. Pursue the richness of life rather than material riches.

God, help us to avoid the temptation of thinking that fame or recognition will lead to prosperity in our lives. The only One we should be concerned about having fame or recognition is You, God. Help us to make Your name known. Today, we pray that Your name is lifted above all other names and that we remember the prosperity that comes through Your grace. Amen.

It is when our things possess us—and thereby replace spiritual reality and the relationship we can experience with God—that they become a problem.

Discovering the supernatural enabling to live with material wealth and still hold fast to the faith may be one of **life's greatest achievements.**

"NOT SO WITH YOU.
INSTEAD, WHOEVER WANTS TO
BECOME GREAT AMONG YOU
MUST BE YOUR SERVANT . . ."

Matthew 20:26 (NIV)

Years ago, after hearing and seeing how much people who faced great loss seemed to love God, I prayed, "Lord, why don't You take everything away from me, so that I can love You more?" He spoke to my heart, saying, "Why? So you will love Me more than *nothing*? No, James, I'm going to bless you greatly so that you can love Me more than *everything!*" And I do! That is the real test—loving God more than everything, instead of loving Him more than nothing.

KEYS TO TRUE PROSPERITY

If true prosperity is not found in material wealth, power, fame, recognition, or comfort, how can we become truly prosperous? Although prosperity ultimately comes from God, there are several things we can do to position ourselves for God's release of blessing in our lives.

In discussing these keys to true prosperity, however, we must understand that the motivation for pursuing these avenues of blessing cannot be purely self-serving. Our focus must be on obedience to God and His Word, not on the expected benefits. We must seek with all of our hearts to live in God's will.

Some of the major keys to prosperity are:

- Walking righteously
- Becoming a giver
- Loving not the world
- Gladly becoming a servant
- Escaping the bondage of debt

The way we conduct our daily lives lays much of the foundation for prosperous living—this is what it means to walk righteously. The ones who will experience true prosperity are those who walk in God's righteousness.

Our motivation in giving should be obedience to God and a loving desire to bless the Lord and other people with the resources that God has entrusted to us. Learning to deny ourselves in order to help others is a vital step toward a meaningful life. Becoming a giver is an important step in experiencing prosperity.

If your heart is set on the things of this world,

you will chase after worldly gain instead of heavenly pursuits. Jesus wants our hearts in the right place, and where we invest our money says volumes about our desires and the focus of our hearts.

One of the fastest ways to find prosperity in our lives is to take on the role of a servant. If we truly assume the attitude and role of Jesus Christ by

> **serving others in humility and grace, we will be truly prosperous in our souls and lives now.**

Perhaps the greatest modern obstacle to "living in giving" is the problem of debt—not just a home mortgage or a regular car payment, but debt that becomes bondage.

When you apply these principles to your life, a lifestyle of true prosperity becomes accessible.

Worry is such a waste of time.
Stop worrying about material
gain and focus your attention on
pursuing the righteousness of God.

The essence of living righteously is walking in God's righteousness rather than one's own, speaking sincerely, telling the truth, rejecting selfishness and unjust gain, refusing to take bribes, and not compromising one's God-given convictions. If we walk righteously, God says, our needs will always be met.

This is true prosperity.

THEREFORE IF THERE IS ANY
ENCOURAGEMENT IN CHRIST, IF THERE IS
ANY CONSOLATION OF LOVE, IF THERE IS
ANY FELLOWSHIP OF THE SPIRIT, IF ANY
AFFECTION AND COMPASSION, MAKE MY
JOY COMPLETE BY BEING OF THE SAME
MIND, MAINTAINING THE SAME LOVE, UNITED
IN SPIRIT, INTENT ON ONE PURPOSE. DO
NOTHING FROM SELFISHNESS OR EMPTY
CONCEIT, BUT WITH HUMILITY OF MIND
REGARD ONE ANOTHER AS MORE IMPORTANT
THAN YOURSELVES; DO NOT MERELY LOOK
OUT FOR YOUR OWN PERSONAL INTERESTS,
BUT ALSO FOR THE INTERESTS OF OTHERS.

Philippians 2:1-4 (NASB)

Dr. Dave Martin shared some wise words on prosperity with us several years ago:

What is prosperity? What does

it mean to be prosperous? Prosperity is simply having enough to do what God calls you to do. It means having enough to survive and to take care of yourself and those who are dependent upon you. But it goes beyond this basic definition to include the ability to thrive—to pursue the dreams that are in your heart and to reach out assisting others with their needs and pursuits. It means having the resources to make a difference and leave an impression on the world. It means having the resources to fulfill the call of God upon your life, with plenty left over for your descendants and for the people and causes God places in your life.

Excerpted from The 12 Traits of the Greats *by Dr. Dave Martin (Harrison House Publishers). Used with permission.*

Remember the story of the Good Samaritan who helped the injured man at the side of the road (see Luke 10:30-37). He didn't put oil on the injured man's wounds hoping to suddenly inherit an oil well. He didn't pay for the man's care at the local inn because he thought he would be rewarded with his own resort hotel. He came to the man's aid because the love of God flowed out of him freely. He was the true good neighbor that Christ says we're to emulate.

The point here is that those who give generously will be blessed generously. God won't shortchange a cheerful giver, but He gives intangible gifts as well as material blessings.

TRUST...

Our trust must be exclusively in Jesus
Christ. He is our provider in every way.
When we trust God as our provider, we
have the peace and comfort that comes
with the belief that all of our needs will
be met. If we know that we will lack for
nothing, as He promises His children,
then we can share His blessing without
worry for ourselves.

Trust makes all the difference!

PRAYER:

Father, lead us to give without focusing on the return. Help us to experience the joy that comes with releasing blessing and provision to the glory of God. Cleanse our hearts and motivations in our giving, God, so that we are approaching it with Christ in mind. Let our actions mirror His words when He said that it is *more blessed to give than to receive.* Amen.

Throughout the Gospels, Jesus puts the primary focus on the joy of giving, not on the return. He offers us the supreme example of what it means to give, in that He gave His life for us, even though He knew there was nothing we could give Him in return. He knew that some would respond to Him, that the return would be people coming to Him in faith. His gift of love was for our sake, for our gain, not His own.

In a similar fashion, God wants us to release every part of ourselves—our love, our time, our money— **for His Kingdom's purpose.**

THEREFORE, AS GOD'S CHOSEN PEOPLE, HOLY
AND DEARLY LOVED, CLOTHE YOURSELVES
WITH COMPASSION, KINDNESS, HUMILITY,
GENTLENESS AND PATIENCE. BEAR WITH EACH
OTHER AND FORGIVE ONE ANOTHER IF ANY
OF YOU HAS A GRIEVANCE AGAINST SOMEONE.
FORGIVE AS THE LORD FORGAVE YOU. AND
OVER ALL THESE VIRTUES PUT ON LOVE, WHICH
BINDS THEM ALL TOGETHER IN PERFECT UNITY.
LET THE PEACE OF CHRIST RULE IN YOUR
HEARTS, SINCE AS MEMBERS OF ONE BODY YOU
WERE CALLED TO PEACE. AND BE THANKFUL . . .

AND WHATEVER YOU DO, WHETHER IN WORD
OR DEED, DO IT ALL IN THE NAME OF THE
LORD JESUS, GIVING THANKS TO GOD THE
FATHER THROUGH HIM.

Colossians 3:12-15, 17 (NIV)

John Bevere, a friend of Life Outreach, shared some insight several years ago on the importance of understanding God's power in and for us. When we understand, the Spirit works in our lives to benefit us and those around us.

Why have we simply not believed what God states in His Word? Our covenant with Him reads, "Now to Him who is able to do exceedingly abundantly above all that we ask or think, according to the power [grace] that works in us" (Ephesians 3:20, NKJV). It is not according to the power that comes periodically from heaven; nor is it according to the power that comes from finding a man and woman who possesses a special ministry gift. No, it is according to *the power that works in us.* Pay particular attention to the front portion of that verse: God is *able.*

I believe God is asking you and me, "Why are you thinking of only what it takes to get by? Why are you merely thinking of you and your family? Why are you not tapping into the full potential I've placed within you and making a significant mark on everyone around you as Daniel did?"

This is why Paul passionately prayed that we might know and understand "what is the immeasurable and unlimited and surpassing greatness of His power in and for us who believe" (Ephesians 1:19, AMP).

Look at Paul's choice of words carefully: *immeasurable, unlimited, surpassing greatness.* When it comes to God's power for your life, what does each of those words mean to you? Notice that Paul is talking of "power *in* us," not power that we might get periodically from a chosen minister if God happens to be feeling good that day. It is also "power *for* us," empowering us to rule in this life. It is power *for* us to rise above and distinguish ourselves so that others can see the evidence for the resurrection power of Jesus Christ! It is power *for* us to shine as bright lights in this dim world.

Excerpted from Relentless: The Power You Need to Never Give Up *by John Bevere (WaterBrook Press).*

. . .

. . . rist's life that we see
. . . o be a true and good
. . . s.

True servants <u>SERVE</u> the interest of
others, not their own.

True servants <u>WORK</u> to make others
successful, not themselves.

True servants <u>REJOICE</u> in the triumphs
of others, not just their own.

And true servants always <u>SACRIFICE</u>
themselves for their master.

God, help us to remember the traits of a servant so that Your Spirit may begin developing servant hearts within us. Your Word tells us that a good servant is patient, kind, self-disciplined, and faithful. And we know that living a Spirit-filled life is essential to godly service. Help us to cultivate these attitudes and attributes in our life so that we may serve others in a fulfilling way. Thank You, Jesus! Amen.

Trust God to supply all of your needs, and allow Him to be God.

We do not dictate the terms by which He answers our prayers, and we should not circumvent His will by getting ourselves into debt bondage trying to answer our own prayers.

LET NO DEBT REMAIN OUTSTANDING,
EXCEPT THE CONTINUING DEBT TO LOVE
ONE ANOTHER, FOR WHOEVER LOVES
OTHERS HAS FULFILLED THE LAW.

Romans 13:8 (NIV)

When personal debt prevents us from helping others, gladly giving to God, or making meaningful choices, we are in bondage. The materialistic mind-set of Western society promotes a "buy it now" mentality that can quickly create a financial prison.

Debt, specifically the type of debt that seeks to enslave, must not be a part of our lives if we wish to be everything that God wants us to be.

WHAT SHOULD WE DO WITH OUR MONEY?

The scriptures tell us several things to do with our money. Interestingly, none of them has to do with selfish motivations or fulfilling our own desires. Instead, they deal in some fashion with helping and caring for others.

For example, 2 Corinthians 9:6-15 (NIV) expounds

the law of sowing and reaping, encouraging believers to give bountifully and cheerfully. The passage makes it clear that God causes His grace to abound so that we may have the means to do good deeds on behalf of others:

> "He who supplies seed to the sower and bread for food will also supply and increase your store of seed and will enlarge the harvest of your righteousness" (v. 10).

Ephesians 4:28 establishes a similar purpose for work and wealth; that is, to help those in need: "He who has been stealing must steal no longer, but must work, doing something useful with his own hands, that he may have something to share with those in need."

Overall, the Bible discusses money in two primary roles: investing and giving. Examples of both uses abound throughout the Old and New Testaments, including instructions on how to succeed in both

do, what not to do, and the proper
toward money.

w Biblical principles that teach us what
to do with our money:

- Tithing
- Caring for our families and others
- Giving
- Investing
- Caring for the poor
- Lending

Jesus tells us that we absolutely must take care of those in need. Those who lack food, water, covering, freedom, and health deserve our help *with no expectation of return.* As Christians, we give out of obedience to Jesus and out of compassion for those who suffer. Both of those reasons merit our gifts. Jesus said to give to those in need, so we give to those in need. In the process, we share God's love.

Jesus' return is promised, as is a great reckoning, and we should work to prepare for that day. Are we using our gifts—spiritual and material—to further His Kingdom? Or are we simply enjoying a comfortable life on our Master's dime? Are we too afraid to step out and invest His wealth in order to expand His influence? Christ compels us to take what He has entrusted to us and invest it wisely so that others may come into His Kingdom. Whether we have been given wisdom, knowledge, talents (aptitudes, skills, and abilities), or money,

we must sow it in good soil —not keep it or hide it; that is, we must put it to good use.

"GIVE TO THE ONE WHO ASKS YOU, AND DO NOT TURN AWAY FROM THE ONE WHO WANTS TO BORROW FROM YOU."

Matthew 5:42 (NIV)

Nancy Alcorn once shared a powerful story about a girl who learned what prosperity looked like in her own life.

After walking through an extremely dark valley, Valerie developed a passion for the Word of God and a desire to understand it deeply. She started setting aside personal time every day to read a section of the Bible and journal about it. Valerie chose her thoughts and chose to meditate on God's Word. That choice brought amazing life and peace, just as the Bible promises.

How many Christians do you know who are saved and go to church but who "walk in the counsel of the ungodly" in their social lives or the entertainment they consume or the kinds of conversations they have at work?

Light dispels the darkness.

As the light of God's Word goes into your mind, it pushes the darkness out. This brings prosperity and success. Then the freedom of Christ begins to connect to your heart in a deeper way.

Living in freedom and getting God's perspective means hiding God's Word in your heart with regular, passionate meditation and memorization.

This is an excerpt from Ditch the Baggage, Change Your Life *by Nancy Alcorn. Copyright ©2015 by Nancy Alcorn. Published by Charisma House. Used by permission.*

CARE...

The principle of caring for our families can be applied spiritually in the sense that we should also care for those in need within the body of Christ. Our heavenly Father blesses those who help take care of His children. As the body of Christ, we should extend the care and love of the Father to those who are in need.

PRAYER:

Father, today we are praying to be good stewards. We know that You own everything, but we are entrusted with our Master's goods. All that we have comes from You, God, and we are called to take care of what we've been given. We are called to share our blessings and be responsible and accountable for what we are entrusted with. Thank You, God, for the opportunity to be stewards of all the good You pour out in our lives. Amen.

We must take care of our family's needs.

However, this does not make a case for a lifestyle of excess. Taking care of our families means providing food, clothing, shelter, and other basic necessities. It does not mean wasting money on frivolous items in order to pacify our selfish desires to accumulate possessions or impress others with our wealth.

GOD DOES NOT INTEND FOR US TO SIMPLY MAINTAIN WHAT HE HAS GIVEN US. WE ARE TO UTILIZE IT . . .

TO EQUIP HIS PEOPLE FOR WORKS OF SERVICE, SO THAT THE BODY OF CHRIST MAY BE BUILT UP.

Ephesians 4:12 (NIV)

Jesus left us what we need to prosper here on earth, but it should be noted that He did not apportion things equally. To one servant, He left five times as much as another. But in the end, they were not judged according to how much they started with or how they competed with each other. They were judged according to what they had done with what was entrusted to them individually.

This is an important truth that must be considered throughout this discussion on prosperity—we must not compare ourselves with others. Some individuals obviously possess more natural talent than others. Some are more gifted, more intelligent, and more fortunate. In this fact we must rejoice.

If we will submit ourselves to God's will and allow Him to use all that He gave us for His glory, then we will find contentment and happiness. When other people accumulate material gain, we must not become jealous. We must rejoice in their success and pray that their focus will remain on God's will.

God is looking at our hearts when we give. And

when we give of the first of our firstfruits or our tithe, God receives and respects that offering. The tithe is your firstfruit. The tithe must be first!

Just as the firstborn and the firstfruits belong to God, so does the tithe belong to Him. But like the other two, it must be first.

The first portion we spend should be the tithe. That is the firstfruit. And according to Exodus 13, that first portion is the redemptive portion. The first portion has the power to redeem the rest. This is the essence of Paul's message in Romans 11:16.

The first portion is the portion that redeems the rest. The first portion carries the blessing. That's why you don't want to give the first portion to the mortgage company. Unfortunately, it seems that many Christians fear the IRS and the mortgage company more than they fear God.

Please keep in mind, I'm not proclaiming the truth about tithing because God needs money; I'm delivering these truths to you for your sake. God doesn't need you to give—you need to be blessed!

Excerpted from The Blessed Life *by Robert Morris (Regal Books).*

TITHE . . .

Tithing is the practice of giving to God the first 10 percent of our earnings. The purpose of the tithe was twofold: to place God in the forefront of people's daily lives and to make sure that nobody lacked for food.

In this way, both great commandments of Christ are expressed: love God and love your neighbor.

Tithing is a way to steward the income God blesses us with.

Lord, today we pray that our love of money never overcomes our love for You. Our money is printed with, "In God We Trust," and we pray that we continue to trust You instead of placing our trust in our money. You are our provider, and it is You who we trust. Amen.

As we accomplish the Lord's purpose on earth,
we become like a watered garden—fruitful.

We become a river of life,

and God says the spring of water will not fail.
We will rebuild the important foundations
in our lives and the lives of those we touch.

"THE LORD WILL GUIDE YOU CONTINUALLY,
AND SATISFY YOUR SOUL IN DROUGHT,
AND STRENGTHEN YOUR BONES;
YOU SHALL BE LIKE A WATERED GARDEN,
AND LIKE A SPRING OF WATER,
WHOSE WATERS DO NOT FAIL."

Isaiah 58:11 (NKJV)

Somewhere there exists a balance between poverty and excess. It is a place where our needs are met, with enough left over to help others. It is a place where we acknowledge that everything belongs to God, who truly owns everything on the earth—a God who is never short of cash and who trusts us to use His wealth to glorify Him 100 percent as His Spirit and His Word direct us.

RELEASING THE RIVER

God has blessed Betty and me tremendously. We've never personally been in the bondage of debt or gone through the financial struggles that many people have experienced. One reason is that we have never sought "stuff." Our philosophy has always been: "Can't afford it? Don't buy it."

I am convinced that our hearts must change until "giving to get" is no longer the major motivating factor in our decisions. **It is only when we have presented ourselves to God as living sacrifices and have committed fully to do His will that He will reveal His perfect will to us.**

In nearly 55 years, Betty and I have never considered the return. We clearly understand "sowing and reaping," but we give to bless others and meet their needs. We find unspeakable joy and blessing when we bless others.

Christian life is not a lottery or spiritual bingo. *Giving is the essence of life and is its own reward.* Jesus wants us to understand this principle. If we release what He has freely given to us, I believe with all my heart that He will supply the increase—not so we can build bigger barns but so we can know what it means to live life abundantly. Those who focus on earthly treasures and on receiving a blessing may get a lot of stuff, but they will not experience fullness of life or fullness of joy. In the end, they will rot in their riches. Possessions do not produce a meaningful life and lasting joy.

The nature of a river is that *whatever it receives, it releases.* That's what makes it a river. With the exception of torrential rain or drought, no matter how much water flows through, it never seems to have more—and no matter how much it releases, it never has less, because everything flows through it and is used to benefit others. Even when it appears ready to overflow its banks, just keep watching, because it is still continuously releasing everything it has received for the purpose of giving life.

If we decide to live our lives like a river—to release everything that God entrusts to us for His eternal purposes—the results will be amazing. What does a river do when it courses through the earth? Everywhere it flows, life springs up.

If we bless, we will be blessed. When we focus on releasing all the resources that God entrusts to us—not storing up bigger things, hanging on, hoarding them up, trying to protect them, trying to guard them, and living in absolute misery—we will experience the joy of abundant living even as we release the flow of abundant life to others. Only then will we actually experience the reality of "God giving us all things richly to enjoy."

Just as the river blesses every place it flows, so too the headwaters spring forth

with abundant life.

So even though the nature of a river is to release its water, the river itself is the first to receive.

"ANYONE WHO BELIEVES IN ME MAY COME AND DRINK! FOR THE SCRIPTURES DECLARE, 'RIVERS OF LIVING WATER WILL FLOW FROM HIS HEART.'"

John 7:38 (NLT)

Sometimes it is hard to wonder how people can live in the kind of suffering that we encounter in the slums of the world. We ask God, "What do You want us to do? The need is so great."

God revealed something to my heart once—and this is the miracle of working in the nations:

God will increase any gift given in His name.

We have seen time and time again how people are so blessed by even the smallest gesture of love. It is not about what you give them, but about the heart with which you give it. It is all about the Father's heart and the expression of the Father's heart. How much more will they not be blessed when they realize that Jesus did something far greater than just giving them a meal, providing fresh water, or educating their children, but that He loves them and cares about them personally!

We know that God wants to do something about the suffering. That is why He makes every outreach possible despite persecution and through the challenges the enemy devises to discourage His church.

God wants to bless all nations beyond our wildest expectations, and He wants us to be a blessing to others.

SOW …

The concept of sowing and reaping is an important aspect of giving. It has to do with the law of the harvest as Paul outlines in 2 Corinthians 9:6-11.

We sow using the seed that God supplies. As a farmer for His Kingdom, we plant in the lives of those around us using the things that we are blessed with.

If we are faithful, Scripture says "in due season" we will reap a harvest. But in order to reap, we must first sow.

God, open our eyes to the needs around us and show us how we can use what You have blessed us with to meet those needs. Show us the water of life that flows through us because of You, and teach us to release the river in Your name. We are so blessed— please show us all of the needs that are waiting to be met. Reveal the ways that we can reach out and touch those who are waiting! Amen.

When we truly delight in the Lord, our hearts' desires will conform to the heart of God. When we place our complete trust in the Lord, including our finances, we can live in comfort and security. When our delight is not in our material possessions or ourselves but in the Lord Himself, then we will discover that God continually gives good gifts to His children.

Our desires will be in line with His desires.

LET US NOT BECOME WEARY IN DOING GOOD,
FOR AT THE PROPER TIME WE WILL REAP A
HARVEST IF WE DO NOT GIVE UP.

Galatians 6:9 (NIV)

One of the things that influenced me greatly in the early days of both my ministry and my marriage was an encounter I had with a family in a church where I conducted a revival. This couple had four children and lived in a modest neighborhood not far from the church.

What caught my attention was their little four-year-old daughter, who'd had her lower leg removed, just below the knee, in a battle with cancer. The mother told me that she had once held a very good job. But as their family grew and their young daughter underwent treatment for cancer, they strongly believed that it was more important to spend time together as a family than to flourish financially.

They realized that the greatest service they could provide to their daughter and to the Lord was to give of their time to care for and love one another.

I learned a valuable lesson in servanthood and witnessed firsthand what I now know as true prosperity.

God is not looking for people who act like Christians. He wants us to be Christians! The word Christian means "anointed or Christlike one." Jesus did not go around "being good"; He went around "doing good" and releasing all who were oppressed. What has He anointed you to do?

If the Spirit of God was placed on Jesus to do all these things, and if we are born of the same Spirit, then we are to do as He did—preach the good news to the poor, set the burdened and battered free, and announce, "This is God's year to act!" (Luke 4:19, MSG) I believe that each and every year is God's year to act, that He is still waiting for us to go into motion on His behalf.

How will you respond when you are fully, dangerously awake? What history will you make? Will you, like the fierce lioness, awaken from a tranquilized state and rise up to defend your family, your community, your world? Are you awake? Even now, what is stirring in your heart?

Excerpted from Lioness Arising *by Lisa Bevere, © 2010 by Lisa Bevere (WaterBrook Press).*

COMMIT . . .

With all my heart I believe that God is looking for people who are committed to His purpose and are living to fulfill His will by blessing others. I believe that God is anxious to pour out the blessings He promises in so many passages of Scripture. When you commit yourself to the Lord, you will clearly see that He is always committed to You!

"A generous person quickly discovers that **each new day provides new opportunities to impact the lives of others.** Every day we can find countless ways—great and small—to make someone's life better."

—*S. Truett Cathy*

TRUST IN THE LORD AND DO GOOD; DWELL
IN THE LAND AND CULTIVATE FAITHFULNESS.
DELIGHT YOURSELF IN THE LORD; AND HE WILL
GIVE YOU THE DESIRES OF YOUR HEART.

Psalm 37:3-4 (NASB)

Have you ever observed a farmer? He prepares the ground, plants the seeds, tends the crop, prays for sun and rain—*and no matter what happens, he will plant again.* The sun may dry up his harvest, the floods may carry it away, or animals may plunder it, but regardless of the outcome, the farmer sows with the hope of reaping a bountiful harvest sometime in the future. Why? Because he is a farmer—he continually invests in the ground, improving it and trusting God for the increase.

OBSTACLES TO
TRUE PROSPERITY

In August 2003, millions of people in the northeast
United States and southeast Canada experienced a
prolonged blackout. With no warning, they lost
power—in some places for days.

Too often we can lose our spiritual "power
connection" as well. Somewhere, something has broken

down. The power that should be ours is gone, and we are left in the dark, trying to guess what went wrong.

Likewise, many things can short-circuit our path to true prosperity. If we don't correct these problems, we are doomed to grope in the dark.

Although the promise of light and energy is there, we will miss it unless our connection to God's power and wisdom is restored.

Consider a regular television set with an aerial antenna. In a large city, we can receive several channels just by plugging the TV in and tuning to the right station.

For purposes of our discussion, let's say that channel 7 is the "true prosperity" channel. It provides twenty-four-hour information on how to be truly prosperous.

There are other channels, too—the "entertainment" channel and the "selfish gain" network. If we are tuned to either of these other channels, we will have the ability to prosper simply by switching to channel 7 and learning the truth, but if we are tuned to the wrong station, we'll get the wrong message.

God is broadcasting truth on channel 7, but too many people are absorbed with entertainment or selfish gain. We must remove the obstacles presented by the other channels and "tune in" to the truth of God if we want to learn how to prosper. His truth is clearly revealed in His Word and is totally trustworthy.

We must never allow anything but God and His will to capture our hearts. If something else captures our hearts, our thoughts, or our passions, it is an idol. For many men and women, their career becomes their idol. When making money or earning status at the workplace becomes more important than the things of God, there can be no true prosperity. Our relationship with God becomes clouded by the idols that stand between us. Idols must be cast down in order for us to prosper.

The fastest way to undermine true prosperity is to fall into the trap of greed. Greed is an excessive or insatiable desire for selfish gain. Do not misinterpret the desire to achieve, succeed, or make gains in life as greed.

All faithful farmers live in faith, trusting God

for the produce and increase according to His will. But working hard for a bountiful harvest does not necessarily indicate greed.

FOR OF THIS YOU CAN BE SURE:
NO IMMORAL, IMPURE OR GREEDY
PERSON—SUCH A PERSON IS AN
IDOLATER—HAS ANY INHERITANCE IN
THE KINGDOM OF CHRIST AND OF GOD.

Ephesians 5:5 (NIV)

Unforgiveness is a cancer. The only way to get rid of it is to cut it out—let go of it. We must not allow the sins and offenses of others to cause us to sin.

There was a time in my marriage when I was dealing with unforgiveness toward my husband. We started going to counseling, and the counselor said, "Let me tell you something. I asked a friend of mine a few weeks ago, who is your favorite person on this earth? My friend replied, 'My tailor.' I said, 'Your tailor? Why would your tailor be your favorite friend?' He said, 'Because every time I go to him he takes fresh measurements.'"

I'm never what I was last week, last month, last year, and this godly man looked at me and said, "Sheila, can you take fresh measurements?"

I said, "Absolutely!"

And I've got to tell you how that has changed our

family. See, that's why Jesus came—because we're all going to mess up. Some of us mess up in ways that are more obvious, but we all mess up.

We're all broken.
We're not fixed.
That's why Christ
gave His own life.

Excerpted from LIFE TODAY *taping with Sheila Walsh, December 14, 2015.*

SELF-CONTROL...

Most people who find themselves in financial distress are there because of one thing: a lack of self-control. One quality imparted by the fullness of the Holy Spirit is self-control, and this is essential in our lives. A lack of self-control leads to debt, and debt kills prosperity. Self-discipline can be difficult, but the Lord respects our efforts to live a self-controlled lifestyle.

Father, today we pray to reject envy. We ask that You take away thoughts of what others have, but we lack. We know that envy takes away peace and joy that comes from You. We ask, instead, that we would learn to enjoy—but never covet—what others have. Help us to rejoice when others are blessed and be at peace with them. Amen.

Materialism makes earthly things the main pursuit of a person's heart. Although the Lord may bless His children with material gifts, much like a loving parent will shower his or her children with Christmas gifts, the love must stay focused on the giver of the gifts, not the gifts themselves.

Our heavenly Father wants us to be thrilled with His *presence*, not just His *presents!*

DO NOT LOVE THE WORLD OR ANYTHING IN
THE WORLD. IF ANYONE LOVES THE WORLD,
LOVE FOR THE FATHER IS NOT IN THEM.

1 John 2:15 (NIV)

What does this phrase "Jesus is enough" actually look like in practical everyday life? Sure, it means we have nothing except Jesus, and all we have is His sustaining grace. But what might that actually look like for us?

When Jesus is enough, we might not actually be poor in the things of this world. We might be relatively wealthy and have cars and houses and college tuition and loving family members and a full refrigerator and a fulfilling job and an abundance of hobbies and clothes and bank accounts and an embarrassment of first-world blessings. And yet we know that if it all disappeared in the next five minutes, Jesus would still be enough.

When Jesus is enough, we might be like that small boy [with five barley loaves and two fish]. We have our health and strength and a bit of provision and dreams of growing up and doing cool things and being a great agent in God's Kingdom and a loving spouse and a caring parent. And we've just been hanging out all day, listening to Jesus, which has been great. And maybe there's a need placed right in front of us. We know we can't ever fill the entire need, because that would take more than all of our resources, maybe half a year's wages, and even then the need wouldn't be filled. But we can still give away our lunch. We can give what we have. We can place our loaves and fishes into the hands of Jesus and trust that He will do with our offering whatever He wants to. That's when Jesus is enough.

When Jesus is enough, we focus on what we have, not what we don't have, and not on what we still might lose. When Jesus is enough, we bless God and don't curse Him. When Jesus is enough, we gaze intently on God and run to Him, not away from Him.

When Jesus is enough, we believe God and don't doubt Him, even though we don't understand our circumstances. When Jesus is enough, we ask Him to take the half of us that's left and make that everything He wants us to be. When Jesus enough, we realize our hearts were made for Jesus, and Jesus isn't just a theological idea—He's a person and not just any person.

Taken from The Comeback *by Louie Giglio. Copyright ©2015 by Louie Giglio. Used by permission of Thomas Nelson. thomasnelson.com.*

SURRENDER...

One of the most striking stories in the Gospels takes place when a powerful, wealthy man asks Jesus what he must do "to inherit eternal life." There was one thing missing in his life—total surrender to Christ, as represented in the area of his money. Before we can arrive at a complete relationship with Christ, we must lay down every obstacle; we must surrender to Him and His will for our lives.

PRAYER:

Father, help us to tune our hearts, our minds, and our spiritual ears to hear and receive wisdom today. We know that Your wisdom clearly speaks to us, yet we do not always listen. Direct our attention to that wisdom and teach us to intently listen to and absorb what You have to share. Amen.

True prosperity is living in God's abiding presence, allowing Him to fulfill His Kingdom purposes through us. When we have truly presented ourselves as living sacrifices, God reveals His good, acceptable, and perfect will. Our yielded lives become lives fulfilled, and lives released—

into true prosperity.

WE NEED TO TUNE OUR SPIRITUAL EARS TO
CLEARLY RECOGNIZE AND HEAR THE VOICE
OF GOD. BY KNOWING GOD'S WRITTEN
WORD, IT IS POSSIBLE TO HEAR HIS CLEARLY
COMMUNICATED SPOKEN WORD. IT HAS
NOTHING TO DO WITH AUDIBLE SOUND; IT HAS
EVERYTHING TO DO WITH SPIRITUAL IMPACT.

I INVITE YOU TO
JOIN ME IN THIS PLEDGE:

Through God's enabling grace, I commit to put Him first above all else and to care for others as I do for myself. I will honor God with the firstfruits of my increase and share my time and talents in ways to benefit others.

In all relationships I will always seek to give more than I could ever receive. I commit to have the heart of a farmer and trust God for the increase—by His means and in His timing. I will joyfully and faithfully give to God's Kingdom, helping the poor and those unable to help me, with no thought of return.

I will make all necessary changes to get out of bondage to debt, even if I must scale way down to ultimately step up. I will begin to live below my means. I will follow wise counsel and seek to tune my spiritual ears to hear the wisdom that comes only from above. I will allow the river of God's life and love to flow freely through me, all to His glory.

BEGIN *NOW* BY FOCUSING ON GOD FIRST.
THEN FIND A NEED AND MEET IT!